101 *Hearty* RECIPES

Santa Fe Sandwiches, page 7

Orange-Peach Dump Cake, page 96

Bouillabaisse Gumbo, page 57

Gooseberry Patch
2500 Farmers Dr., #110
Columbus, OH 43235

www.gooseberrypatch.com

1•800•854•6673

Copyright 2011, Gooseberry Patch 978-1-936283-71-2
First Printing, June, 2011

Gooseberry Patch *cookbooks*

German-Style Short Ribs, page 63

Bratwurst & Potato Salad, page 62

Since 1992, we've been publishing our own country cookbooks for every kitchen and for every meal of the day! Each title has hundreds of budget-friendly recipes, using ingredients you already have on hand in your pantry.

In addition, you'll find helpful tips and ideas on every page, along with our hand-drawn artwork and plenty of personality. Their lay-flat binding makes them so easy to use...they're sure to become a fast favorite in your kitchen.

Call us toll-free at

1•800•854•6673

and we'd be delighted to tell you all about our newest titles!

Shop with us online anytime at

www.gooseberrypatch.com

Send us your favorite recipe!

*and the memory that makes it special for you!** If we select your recipe for a brand-new **Gooseberry Patch** cookbook, your name will appear right along with it...and you'll receive a FREE copy of the book!

Submit your recipe on our website at
www.gooseberrypatch.com

Or mail to:

Gooseberry Patch • Attn: Cookbook Dept.
2500 Farmers Dr., #110 • Columbus, OH 43235

*Please include the number of servings and all other necessary information!

Have a taste for more?

Visit **www.gooseberrypatch.com** to join our **Circle of Friends**!

- Free recipes, tips and ideas plus a complete cookbook index
- Get special email offers and our monthly eLetter delivered to your inbox
- Find local stores with **Gooseberry Patch** cookbooks, calendars and organizers

Nacho Chicken Dip, page 11

Crunchy Oat & Fruit Crisp, page 93

Marinated Carrot Salad, page 12

Black Bean & Rice Enchiladas, page 56

Weda's Stuffed Tomatoes, page 26
The Best Pot Roast Ever, page 81
Raspberry Upside-Down Cake, page 89

CONTENTS

Fun & Filling 7

Speedy & Satisfying 30

Casual & Comforting............... 56

Baked & Buttery 82

Apple Blush Pie, page 85

Dedication

For every family who loves passing homestyle dishes around the table!

Appreciation

To those who shared their best recipes for serving up satisfaction, thank you!

Meatloaf Mexicana, page 61

Santa Fe Sandwiches

6 hoagie buns, split
1/2 c. mayonnaise
1/2 c. sour cream
1/2 t. chili powder
1/2 t. ground cumin
1/4 t. salt
6 tomatoes, sliced
8-oz. pkg. deli sliced turkey
1/2 c. sliced black olives
1/3 c. green onions, sliced
3 avocados, pitted, peeled and sliced
8-oz. pkg. shredded Cheddar cheese
Garnish: shredded lettuce and salsa

Arrange hoagie buns open-faced on an ungreased baking sheet; set aside. In a bowl, mix together mayonnaise, sour cream and seasonings; spread over each bun. Equally layer remaining ingredients except garnish in the order listed; bake at 350 degrees for 15 minutes. Garnish with lettuce and salsa. Makes 12 servings.

Deanne Birkestrand
Minden, NE

Add a fresh fruit salad for a quick & tasty meal with friends.

Fun & Filling

Corn Chip Salad

1 head lettuce, shredded
6 to 8 eggs, hard-boiled, peeled and sliced
1-1/2 c. shredded Colby cheese
16-oz. pkg. bacon, crisply cooked and crumbled
4 to 6 c. corn chips, broken into smaller pieces

Combine all ingredients in a large serving bowl. Just before serving, add Dressing to salad and toss. Makes 6 to 8 servings.

Dressing:

1 c. mayonnaise
2 T. vinegar
1/4 c. milk
1/4 c. sugar
1/4 c. brown sugar, packed

Whisk together all ingredients until combined.

Easy French Dip Sandwiches

4 lbs. stew beef, cubed
2 onions, halved
4 cloves garlic
2 10-1/2 oz. cans beef broth
4 c. water
4 t. beef bouillon granules
sandwich buns, split

Combine all ingredients except buns in a slow cooker. Cover and cook on low setting for 8 to 10 hours. Discard onions and garlic. Remove beef to a bowl and shred; spoon onto buns. Serve with beef juices from slow cooker for dipping. Serves 18 to 20.

Kathy White
Cato, NY

My husband is the pastor of our church and our family of ten regularly hosts meals with the congregation. These hearty sandwiches feed a crowd!

Deluxe Cocktail Sausages

Carrie Helke
Schofield, WI

A deliciously sweet and savory appetizer...a perfect start to any get-together!

1/2 c. butter
3 T. brown sugar, packed
3 T. honey
1/2 c. chopped pecans
8-oz. tube refrigerated crescent rolls, separated
24 smoked cocktail sausages

Preheat oven to 400 degrees. As oven is warming, melt butter in oven in a 13"x9" glass baking pan. When butter is melted, add brown sugar, honey and pecans; stir to coat bottom of the pan. Slice each crescent roll triangle into thirds. Roll each smaller triangle around one sausage. Place on butter mixture, seam-side down. Bake, uncovered, at 400 degrees for 15 minutes, or until golden. Makes 2 dozen.

Nacho Chicken Dip

16-oz. can refried beans
12-oz. can chicken, drained
16-oz. jar chunky salsa
8-oz. pkg. shredded Mexican-blend cheese
tortilla chips

Layer beans, chicken, salsa and cheese in a lightly greased one-quart casserole dish. Bake, uncovered, at 350 degrees for 30 minutes, or until cheese is bubbly. Serve hot with tortilla chips. Makes about 6-1/2 cups.

Trudy Williams
Middlesex, NC

We love this delicious dip at parties...it's even good as a meal, paired with a side salad.

Marinated Carrot Salad

Jill Ball
Highland, UT

This colorful side dish is always the first to go wherever I take it!

2 lbs. carrots, peeled and sliced
3 green onions, chopped
1/2 c. green pepper, chopped
10-3/4 oz. can tomato soup
1/2 c. oil
3/4 c. sugar
1/2 c. vinegar
1 T. Worcestershire sauce
1 t. salt
1/8 t. cayenne pepper

Place vegetables in a bowl; set aside. In a saucepan, combine remaining ingredients. Bring to a boil over medium heat, stirring constantly. Pour over vegetables. Cover and refrigerate for 24 hours before serving. Serve chilled. Serves 6 to 8.

Tailgate Sandwich Ring

2 11-oz. tubes refrigerated French bread dough
1/2 lb. bacon, crisply cooked and crumbled
3/4 c. mayonnaise
1 T. green onions, chopped
1/2 lb. deli sliced turkey
1/2 lb. deli sliced ham
1/2 lb. sliced provolone cheese
2 tomatoes, sliced
2 c. lettuce, chopped

Spray a Bundt® pan with non-stick vegetable spray. Place both tubes of dough into pan, seam-side up, joining ends together to form one large ring. Pinch edges to seal tightly. Lightly spray top of dough with non-stick vegetable spray. Bake at 350 degrees for 40 to 45 minutes, until golden. Carefully turn out; cool completely. Combine bacon, mayonnaise and onions; mix well. Slice bread horizontally. Spread half the bacon mixture over bottom half of bread. Top with turkey, ham and provolone. Place on an ungreased baking sheet. Bake at 350 degrees for 5 minutes, or until cheese melts. Top with tomatoes and lettuce. Spread remaining bacon mixture on top half of bread; place over lettuce. Slice into wedges. Serves 8.

Crystal Vogel
Springdale, PA

I make this for every tailgating party...my husband and friends request it all the time.

4-Layer Cookie Bars

16-oz. pkg. rectangular buttery crackers
1/2 c. margarine
2/3 c. sugar
1/2 c. brown sugar, packed
1 c. graham cracker crumbs
1/4 c. milk
2/3 c. creamy peanut butter
1/2 c. semi-sweet chocolate chips
1/2 c. peanut butter chips

Line the bottom of a buttered 13"x9" baking pan with a single layer of crackers; set aside. Melt margarine in a heavy saucepan; add sugars, graham cracker crumbs and milk. Heat over medium-high heat until sugars dissolve, stirring often; spread over crackers in pan. Arrange another single layer of crackers on top; set aside. Combine remaining ingredients in a saucepan; heat over low heat until melted, stirring until smooth and creamy. Spread over crackers; set aside until firm. Cut into bars to serve. Makes 2 dozen.

Sandwich on a Stick

1/2 lb. deli ham, cubed
1/2 lb. deli turkey, cubed
1/2 lb. deli chicken, cubed
1/2 lb. Cheddar cheese, cubed
4 c. bread, cubed
1 pt. cherry tomatoes
4 dill pickles, cut into 1-inch pieces
8 wooden skewers
Garnish: mustard, spicy brown mustard, mayonnaise

Alternate all ingredients except condiments onto skewers. Garnish as desired. Makes 8.

Amy Hunt
Traphill, NC

Here's a simple snack to make for a picnic or party. Adjust the quantity and ingredients to suit your family's tastes.

Red Velvet Cake Balls

18-1/2 oz. pkg. red velvet cake mix
16-oz. container cream cheese frosting
16-oz. pkg. regular or white melting chocolate

Prepare and bake cake mix following package directions for a 13"x9" cake; let cool. Crumble cooled cake into a large bowl. Stir in cream cheese frosting. Roll mixture into balls the size of quarters. Place on baking sheets and chill for several hours or overnight. Melt chocolate in a double boiler. Dip cake balls into chocolate and place on wax paper. Let sit until firm. Makes about 4 dozen.

Sangria Punch

3/4 c. sweetened lemonade drink mix
4 c. cranberry juice cocktail
1 c. orange juice
1 T. lime juice
3 c. club soda, chilled
2 oranges, sliced
2 limes, sliced

Empty drink mix into a large pitcher. Add juices, stirring until drink mix is completely dissolved. Refrigerate until ready to serve. At serving time, stir in club soda and fruit. Makes 8 servings.

Sheila Gwaltney
Johnson City, TN

I served this refreshing punch at a Cinco de Mayo party. It was a total hit! So easy to double...try it with pink lemonade too.

Spiced Orange Pecans

Debi DeVore
Dover, OH

A tasty hostess gift that's sure to be welcome.

2 egg whites, beaten
3 T. orange juice
2 c. pecan halves
1-1/2 c. powdered sugar
2 T. cornstarch
1 T. orange zest
1 t. cinnamon
3/4 t. ground cloves
1/4 t. allspice
1/8 t. salt

In a bowl, combine egg whites and orange juice. Add pecans and toss to coat; drain. In a separate bowl, combine remaining ingredients. Add pecans and toss to coat. Spread in a single layer in a greased 15"x10" jelly-roll pan. Bake at 250 degrees for 30 to 35 minutes, until dry and lightly golden. Cool completely; store in an airtight container. Makes about 3-1/2 cups.

Fun & Filling

Ranch Chicken Pizza

2 12-inch ready-to-use pizza crusts
16-oz. jar Alfredo sauce
2-oz. pkg. ranch salad dressing mix
4 c. shredded mozzarella cheese, divided
8-oz. pkg. grilled chicken strips, coarsely chopped
2.8-oz. pkg. ready-to-use bacon, crumbled
1 red onion, thinly sliced
1 green pepper, sliced into thin strips
3 roma tomatoes, thinly sliced
Garnish: grated Parmesan cheese

If package directs, bake pizza crusts for a few minutes. In a small bowl, combine Alfredo sauce and salad dressing mix. Divide between 2 crusts, spreading evenly. Top each pizza with 2 cups mozzarella cheese. On each pizza, arrange half of the remaining ingredients except garnish. Sprinkle with Parmesan cheese. Bake at 425 degrees for 20 minutes, or until crust is lightly golden and cheese is bubbly. Makes 2 pizzas; 6 servings each.

Lorrie Smith
Drummonds, TN

This is my version of a local favorite. Quicker than delivery!

Sweet Salsa

Traci Doxtator
Henderson, NV

My friend Marcia and I have had such fun entertaining each other's families every weekend...and we've built the most special friendship over salsa, chips and a deck of cards!

2 c. cantaloupe, peeled, seeded and finely chopped
2 c. cherry tomatoes, chopped
1/4 c. green onions, chopped
1/4 c. fresh basil, chopped
2 T. jalapeños, diced
2 T. lime juice
2 T. orange juice
1/4 t. salt
1/8 t. pepper
tortilla chips

Stir together all ingredients except chips; cover and refrigerate for at least 30 minutes. Serve with chips. Makes about 4-3/4 cups.

Brown Sugar Barbecue Sandwiches

1 c. water
3/4 c. catsup
2 T. brown sugar, packed
1 onion, chopped
2 T. mustard
1 T. chili powder
2 t. salt
1 t. pepper
2 lbs. lean ground beef
12 sandwich buns, split

In a large saucepan, mix all ingredients except beef and buns. Bring to a boil over medium heat. Add uncooked beef; simmer for 30 minutes. Spoon onto buns. Makes 12 servings.

Kathy Majeske
Denver, PA

There are many recipes for making barbecues, but this one has been in my family for as long as I can remember. There's no need to brown the ground beef first.

Game-Time Party Mix

- 2 c. bite-size crispy corn cereal squares
- 2 c. mini pretzels
- 1 c. peanuts
- 1 c. caramels, unwrapped and coarsely chopped
- 11-oz. pkg. butterscotch chips

Combine cereal, pretzels, peanuts and caramels in a large bowl. In a microwave-safe bowl, microwave butterscotch chips on medium power for one minute; stir. Microwave an additional 15 seconds and stir; repeat until melted and smooth. Pour over cereal mixture; stir to coat evenly. Spread mixture into a 13"x9" baking pan coated with non-stick vegetable spray. Let stand 20 minutes, or until firm. Break into small pieces. Makes about 6 cups.

Fun & Filling

Buffalo Wing Dip

- 2 8-oz. pkgs. cream cheese, softened
- 15-oz. jar chunky blue cheese salad dressing
- 2 boneless, skinless chicken breasts, cooked and shredded
- 12-oz. bottle chicken wing sauce
- 8-oz. pkg. shredded Monterey Jack and Cheddar cheese blend
- tortilla chips or crackers

In a bowl, blend together cream cheese and salad dressing until smooth. Spread in the bottom of an ungreased 8"x8" baking pan. Combine chicken and wing sauce; spoon over cream cheese mixture. Sprinkle with shredded cheese. Bake, uncovered, at 350 degrees for 20 minutes, or until cheese is melted and dip is heated through. Serve with tortilla chips or crackers. Serves 10.

Amanda Coomer
Franklin, OH

Every time I take this zesty dip somewhere, I come home with an empty pan!

Hot Chicken Sandwiches

Kelly Patrick
Gallipolis, OH

I found this in an old garden club cookbook and have been making it for at least twenty years. People think it sounds strange, but when they taste it, they want the recipe!

6-oz. pkg. chicken-flavored stuffing mix
6-oz. pkg. herb-flavored stuffing mix
12-1/2 oz. can chicken, drained and flaked
10-3/4 oz. can cream of chicken soup
sandwich buns, split

In a stockpot, prepare stuffing mixes as packages direct. Mix in chicken and soup. Increase heat to medium; cook and stir until heated through. Serve on buns. Serves 8 to 10.

Aunt Louise's Salad

Virginia Craven
Denton, TX

My Aunt Louise is a wonderful self-taught southern cook. In her eighties, she still entertains and is our family's inspiration in the kitchen!

8 c. salad greens, torn
12 slices bacon, crisply cooked and crumbled
1 c. crumbled blue or feta cheese
10-oz. pkg. frozen peas, thawed
3/4 to 1 c. sweetened dried cranberries
1/2 c. green onions, chopped
1 c. whole cashews

Mix salad greens in a serving bowl. Arrange remaining ingredients except cashews in a pie shape to cover greens. Cover and chill until serving time. Toss salad with desired amount of Balsamic Dressing; sprinkle cashews on top and serve with additional dressing on the side. Serves 10 to 12.

Balsamic Dressing:

1 c. balsamic vinegar
1/2 c. maple syrup
1/4 c. green onions, minced
2 t. seasoned salt
2 t. seasoned pepper
1/2 t. garlic, minced
2-1/2 c. olive oil

Combine all ingredients in a food processor. Process until smooth.

Weda's Stuffed Tomatoes

Weda Mosellie
Phillipsburg, NJ

A pop-in-your-mouth snack that will go fast at your next party.

10 roma tomatoes, halved lengthwise
1/2 c. shredded mozzarella cheese
1/2 c. crumbled feta cheese
1 T. olive oil
pepper to taste
Optional: bread crumbs

Scoop out insides of tomato halves; discard. In a bowl, mix cheeses together; carefully spoon into tomato halves. Arrange tomatoes in a lightly greased 13"x9" baking pan. Drizzle oil over tomatoes; sprinkle with pepper and bread crumbs, if using. Bake, uncovered, at 375 degrees for 15 to 20 minutes. Makes 20 servings.

Fun & Filling

Berry Patch Fondue

Robin Hill
Rochester, NY

Use any combination of fresh or frozen berries in this scrumptious alternative to chocolate fondue.

1-1/2 lbs. raspberries and strawberries, hulled
1/4 c. sugar
pound cake, cubed

Place berries in a blender and process until smooth. Press mixture through a strainer or cheesecloth and into a saucepan. Add sugar and cook over medium heat until sugar has dissolved. Transfer to a warm fondue pot; keep warm. Serve with pound cake cubes for dipping. Serves 6.

Peanut Buttery Chocolatey Cups

Lana Rulevish
Ashley, IL

Yummy bites that can be made with creamy or crunchy peanut butter. They always go fast on a cookie tray!

16-oz. pkg. melting chocolate
1 c. creamy peanut butter
2 c. powdered sugar
1 c. graham cracker crumbs
1/2 c. butter, softened

Melt half the chocolate in a double boiler. For each cup, spoon one teaspoon melted chocolate into bottom of a mini paper cupcake liner; refrigerate until firm. In a medium bowl, combine remaining ingredients; stir well. Press one teaspoon peanut butter mixture over chocolate, pressing to edges of liner. Melt remaining chocolate. Spoon melted chocolate over peanut butter to cover; refrigerate until firm. Makes about 8 dozen.

Cornbread Salad

8-1/2 oz. pkg. cornbread mix
ranch salad dressing to taste
15-1/2 oz. can black beans, drained and rinsed
15-oz. can corn, drained
2-1/4 oz. can sliced black olives, drained
2 tomatoes, chopped
1 red onion, chopped
1/2 c. green onions, chopped
2/3 c. shredded Cheddar cheese
1/2 lb. bacon, crisply cooked and crumbled

Prepare and bake cornbread according to package directions. When cool, crumble cornbread and sprinkle half in the bottom of a large serving dish. Pour enough salad dressing over the bread to make a smooth covering. Layer the beans, corn and olives over the dressing. Next layer tomatoes, onions, cheese and bacon. Sprinkle remaining cornbread crumbs over top. Cover and refrigerate until serving time. Serves 8 to 10.

Diana Krol
Nickerson, KS

A layered salad that's especially nice for family and church gatherings like picnics and BBQs. Try it with pinto beans if you like.

Roasted Chicken & Apples

5 c. apples, peeled, cored and chopped
1 t. fresh sage, chopped
1/4 t. cinnamon
1/8 t. nutmeg
4 cloves garlic, chopped
1/2 t. salt, divided
8 skinless chicken thighs
1/4 t. pepper

In a large bowl, combine first 5 ingredients with 1/4 teaspoon salt; toss well to coat. Spread on a 15"x10" jelly-roll pan sprayed with non-stick vegetable spray. Season chicken with remaining salt and pepper; arrange on top of apple mixture. Bake, uncovered, at 475 degrees for 25 minutes, or until juices run clear when chicken is pierced with a fork. Makes 8 servings.

Cathy Hillier
Salt Lake City, UT

My family gets so excited for dinner when they smell the spicy aroma coming from the kitchen!

Peppers & Pierogies

10-oz. pkg. frozen potato and onion pierogies
16-oz. pkg. frozen stir-fry peppers and onions
8-oz. can tomato sauce
salt and pepper to taste

Cook pierogies according to package directions. Drain, reserving 1/2 cup of cooking liquid; cover pierogies to keep warm. Spray a large skillet with non-stick vegetable spray. Add frozen vegetables; cook until tender and golden and most of the liquid is cooked off. Stir in tomato sauce and reserved liquid; heat through. Toss vegetable mixture with pierogies; season with salt and pepper. Serves 3 to 4.

Cat Bonacchi
Levittown, NY

Makes a satisfying meatless main, or serve with grilled sausages for an even heartier supper.

Speedy & Satisfying

Chicken & Barley Chili

Renae Scheiderer
Beallsville, OH

I found this recipe and adjusted it a bit to our family's taste. I'm happy to report that it's a hit!

14-1/2 oz. can diced tomatoes
16-oz. jar salsa
14-1/2 oz. can chicken broth
1 c. pearled barley, uncooked
3 c. water
1 T. chili powder
1 t. ground cumin
15-oz. can kidney beans, drained and rinsed
15-1/4 oz. can corn, drained
3 c. cooked chicken breast, cut into bite-size pieces
Optional: shredded Cheddar cheese, sour cream

In a stockpot, combine undrained tomatoes, salsa, broth, barley, water and seasonings. Bring to a boil over high heat. Cover and reduce heat to low; simmer for 20 minutes, stirring occasionally. Add beans, corn and chicken. Increase heat to high; bring to a boil. Cover and reduce heat to low. Simmer for another 5 minutes, or until barley is tender. Ladle into bowls. Top with cheese and sour cream, if desired. Serves 8 to 10.

7th-Heaven Layered Salad

8-oz. pkg. cream cheese, softened
1 c. mayonnaise
1 c. sour cream
1 t. dried basil
1/2 t. garlic powder
1/2 t. onion powder
1/2 head lettuce, torn
2 tomatoes, chopped
1 cucumber, sliced
3 carrots, peeled and sliced
10 to 12 green onions, finely chopped
8-oz. pkg. shredded sharp Cheddar cheese
1 lb. bacon, crisply cooked and crumbled

Blend together cream cheese, mayonnaise, sour cream and seasonings; cover and set aside. Layer lettuce, tomatoes, cucumber, carrots and onions in a glass trifle dish or 13"x9" glass baking pan; spoon cream cheese mixture over top. Sprinkle with Cheddar cheese and bacon. Cover and refrigerate until serving time. Serves 12.

Sassy Squash

Annette Ingram
Grand Rapids, MI

My neighbor Jenny is kind enough to share the bounty of her garden. I make sure to keep stewed tomatoes in the pantry when squash are in season!

1/2 c. red onion, sliced thin
1 T. butter
3 c. yellow squash, sliced thin
3 c. zucchini, sliced thin
1 t. salt
pepper to taste
1 clove garlic, minced
16-oz. can stewed tomatoes

In a large skillet, sauté onion in butter over medium-high heat for 2 minutes. Stir in remaining ingredients except tomatoes. Reduce heat to medium and cook until crisp-tender. Add tomatoes and cook until heated through. Serves 6 to 8.

Fancy Crescent Chicken

Roberta Scheeler
Ashley, OH

The flakiness of the rolls and the convenience of buying them in a package can't be beat!

3-oz. pkg. cream cheese, softened
3 T. butter, softened
10-oz. can chicken, drained
1/4 t. salt
1/8 t. pepper
2 T. milk
1 T. fresh chives, chopped
1 T. onion, chopped
1 T. chopped pimentos
2 8-oz. tubes refrigerated crescent rolls
2 T. butter, melted
3/4 c. seasoned croutons, crushed

In a bowl, mix together cream cheese and softened butter until smooth. Mix in chicken, salt, pepper, milk, chives, onion and pimentos. Separate crescent rolls into rectangles. Spoon chicken mixture over each rectangle. Fold dough over and press together to seal edges. Brush with melted butter and sprinkle with croutons. Arrange on ungreased baking sheets. Bake at 350 degrees for 20 to 25 minutes, until golden. Serves 8.

Bowties & Blush

16-oz. pkg. bowtie pasta, uncooked
1 T. butter
1 onion, chopped
1 banana pepper, chopped
2 cloves garlic, chopped
1 T. all-purpose flour
3/4 c. milk
1/2 c. whipping cream
1/2 t. salt
1-1/4 c. spaghetti sauce
1/4 c. grated Parmesan cheese
1/4 c. fresh basil, chopped

Cook pasta according to package directions; drain. Meanwhile, melt butter over medium heat in a large skillet; add onion, pepper and garlic. Sauté until tender; stir in flour. Gradually add milk, cream and salt; bring to a boil. Mix in spaghetti sauce; reduce heat and simmer 10 minutes. Remove from heat; pour into a serving bowl. Add pasta; mix gently. Sprinkle with Parmesan cheese and basil; serve warm. Serves 8.

Sam's Sweet-and-Sour Pork

Sharon Tillman
Hampton, VA

My best friend Samantha shared this with me. A tasty dish that cooks up in a snap!

1 T. oil
1 lb. boneless pork loin, cut into 1/2-inch cubes
1 c. onion, chopped
1 c. green pepper, cut into 3/4-inch cubes
1 c. red pepper, cut into 3/4-inch cubes
1 t. garlic, minced
8-oz. can pineapple chunks, drained
1 c. catsup
1 T. brown sugar, packed
1 T. white vinegar
1/2 t. salt
1/4 t. pepper
cooked rice

Heat oil in a large skillet; brown pork on both sides. Add onion, peppers and garlic; cook and stir 5 minutes. Drain; add remaining ingredients except rice. Cover and simmer 10 minutes, or until pork is tender. Serve over hot rice. Serves 6 to 8.

Speedy & Satisfying

Quick & Creamy Vegetable Soup

3/4 c. butter, softened
3/4 c. all-purpose flour
2 c. half-and-half, warmed
6 c. vegetable or chicken broth, warmed and divided
2 to 3 c. frozen mixed vegetables, thawed
Garnish: dried parsley

Combine butter and flour in a large saucepan over medium heat. Cook and stir until butter is melted. Add half-and-half; stir until smooth and slightly thickened. Stir in 2 cups broth. Cook over low heat until blended and heated through, about 4 minutes. Add remaining broth and vegetables. Heat through without boiling until vegetables are tender. Ladle into bowls; sprinkle with parsley. Serves 6 to 8.

Salmon with Balsamic Sauce

4 salmon fillets
1/2 t. salt
1/4 t. pepper
2 t. oil
1/4 c. water
1/4 c. balsamic vinegar
4-1/2 t. lemon juice
4 t. brown sugar, packed

Sprinkle both sides of fillets with salt and pepper. In a skillet, cook salmon in oil over medium heat for 10 to 15 minutes, until fish flakes easily with a fork. Meanwhile, combine water, vinegar, lemon juice and brown sugar in a small saucepan. Bring to a boil; cook until liquid is reduced to about 1/3 cup. Serve over salmon. Serves 4.

Cajun Oven Fries

3 to 4 T. olive oil
2 T. hot pepper sauce
1 t. dried thyme
1 t. ground cumin
1 t. paprika
4 potatoes, cut into wedges
salt and pepper to taste

Combine oil, hot sauce and seasonings in a large bowl; toss with potatoes. Arrange potatoes in a single layer on an ungreased non-stick baking sheet. Sprinkle with salt and pepper. Bake at 450 degrees for 20 minutes, turning once, until tender. Serves 4.

Speedy & Satisfying

Open-Faced Lone Star Burgers

Angie Venable
Gooseberry Patch

I first saw a chicken version of this recipe on the cover of a magazine. I decided to make it with burgers instead. Yum!

1/4 c. onion, chopped
2 cloves garlic, minced
1/4 t. dried thyme
1-1/2 c. shredded Colby Jack cheese, divided
1-1/2 lbs. ground beef
6 slices frozen garlic Texas toast
8-oz. can tomato sauce
1 T. brown sugar, packed
1 t. Worcestershire sauce
1 t. steak sauce

In a large bowl, combine onion, garlic, thyme and one cup cheese. Crumble beef over top and mix well. Form into 6 oval-shaped patties. In a large skillet, cook patties over medium heat for 5 to 6 minutes per side, to desired doneness. Meanwhile, prepare toast according to package directions. Drain patties; set aside and keep warm. Add remaining ingredients to the skillet. Bring to a boil; cook and stir for 2 minutes, or until slightly thickened. Return burgers to skillet; turn to coat. Sprinkle with remaining cheese. Serve burgers on toast. Makes 6 servings.

Dijon Chicken & Fresh Herbs

Stacie Avner
Delaware, OH

I love making this family favorite in the summertime when my garden is full of fresh herbs!

4 to 6 boneless, skinless chicken breasts
1 t. kosher salt
1 t. pepper
3 to 4 T. Dijon mustard
2 T. fresh rosemary, minced
2 T. fresh thyme, minced
2 T. fresh parsley, minced

Sprinkle chicken with salt and pepper. Grill over medium-high heat 5 to 6 minutes per side, or until juices run clear. Remove from grill and brush both sides with mustard; sprinkle with herbs. Serves 4 to 6.

Tangy Summer Slaw

1 head red cabbage, shredded
1 head green cabbage, shredded
1 carrot, peeled and shredded
1 onion, finely chopped
1 green pepper, finely chopped
16-oz. bottle red wine vinegar & oil salad dressing
1/4 c. olive oil
1/4 c. sugar
1 T. Dijon mustard
1 t. caraway seed
salt and pepper to taste

Toss together vegetables in a large serving bowl; set aside. Combine remaining ingredients; pour over vegetables. Refrigerate until ready to serve. Toss before serving. Makes 8 to 10 servings.

Texas Two-Step in a Jar

1/2 lb. ground beef
1.6-oz. pkg. brown gravy mix
2 T. chili powder
2 t. dried oregano
1 t. ground cumin
1 t. dried, minced onion
1 t. garlic salt
10 to 12 tortilla chips, coarsely crushed
1-1/4 c. wagon wheel pasta, uncooked
7 c. water
15-oz. can corn
16-oz. can diced tomatoes
Garnish: additional tortilla chips, shredded Monterey Jack cheese

Brown ground beef in a large saucepan; drain. Add remaining ingredients except corn, tomatoes and garnish; bring to a boil. Stir in corn and tomatoes. Reduce heat; cover and simmer for 20 to 25 minutes until pasta is tender. Garnish with tortilla chips and cheese. Serves 8.

Jo Ann

How fun! Spoon gravy mix into a one-pint wide-mouth jar. Combine the seasonings and pour over gravy mix. Add tortilla chips and pasta to fill jar; secure lid. Tie on a tag with cooking instructions.

Instructions:

Brown 1/2 pound ground beef in a large saucepan. Add jar contents and 7 cups of water; bring to a boil. Stir in 15-ounce can corn and 16-ounce can chopped tomatoes. Reduce heat, cover and simmer for 20 to 25 minutes until pasta is tender. Garnish with tortilla chips and shredded Monterey Jack cheese. Serves 8.

Bavarian Beef & Noodles

Janie Branstetter
Duncan, OK

This is a hearty casserole the whole family will enjoy. You won't be disappointed!

8-oz. pkg. egg dumpling noodles
1 lb. ground beef
2 8-oz. cans tomato sauce
1 t. salt
1/4 t. garlic salt
1/8 t. pepper
2 c. sour cream
1/2 c. green onions, sliced
1 c. shredded Cheddar cheese

Cook noodles according to package directions; drain and set aside. Meanwhile, brown ground beef in a skillet over medium heat; drain. Stir in tomato sauce, salt, garlic salt and pepper. In a bowl, combine sour cream, onions and noodles. In a greased 2-quart casserole dish, alternate layers of noodle mixture and beef mixture, ending with beef. Sprinkle cheese over top. Bake, uncovered, at 350 degrees for 20 to 25 minutes. Serves 4 to 6.

Speedy Goulash

8-oz. pkg. elbow macaroni, uncooked
1 lb. ground beef
1 onion
2 cloves garlic
1 T. paprika
1-1/2 t. ground coriander
1-1/2 t. ground cumin
1/4 t. nutmeg
14-1/2 oz. can diced tomatoes
3 T. sour cream
salt and pepper to taste

Cook macaroni according to package directions; drain. Meanwhile, brown ground beef in a large skillet over medium heat. While beef is cooking, grate onion and garlic directly into beef. Add spices and mix well. When beef is just cooked, drain. Add undrained tomatoes; warm through. Stir in sour cream, salt, pepper and cooked macaroni; serve immediately. Serves 6.

Farmhouse Chicken Bake

8-oz. pkg. elbow macaroni, uncooked
4 green onions, sliced
2 T. butter, melted and divided
2 T. all-purpose flour
1-1/2 c. milk
1/2 c. chicken broth
4 c. cooked chicken, cubed
salt to taste
1/4 t. pepper
1/2 t. dried thyme
1 c. shredded Cheddar cheese
1 c. frozen peas, thawed
8 slices bacon, crisply cooked and crumbled
1 c. dry bread crumbs

Cook macaroni according to package directions; drain. Meanwhile, in a skillet over medium-low heat, cook onions in one tablespoon melted butter for one minute. Stir in flour until smooth. Gradually stir in milk and broth, cooking and stirring until slightly thickened. Stir in chicken, seasonings, cheese, peas and bacon. Mix in macaroni. Spoon into a greased 3-quart casserole dish. Combine bread crumbs with remaining butter; sprinkle over top. Bake, uncovered, at 350 degrees for 25 to 30 minutes, until golden. Serves 6.

Mom's One-Pot Pork Chop Dinner

Kim Allen
New Albany, IN

A dinner classic for good reason! Simple to prepare and so comforting.

1 T. butter
4 pork chops
3 potatoes, peeled and sliced
2 c. baby carrots
1 onion, sliced
10-3/4 oz. can cream of mushroom soup
1/4 c. water

Melt butter in a skillet over medium heat; brown pork chops for 3 to 5 minutes on each side. Add potatoes, carrots and onion to skillet. In a bowl, combine soup and water; add to skillet. Cover and simmer for 15 to 20 minutes, until vegetables are tender. Makes 4 servings.

Hoppin' Jane

4 slices bacon, coarsely chopped
1/2 c. onion, chopped
1/4 c. celery, chopped
1/4 c. red pepper, chopped
2 cloves garlic, pressed
16-oz. can black-eyed peas, drained
1-1/4 c. instant rice, uncooked
1 c. water
1 c. chicken broth
salt and pepper to taste

In a skillet over medium-high heat, cook bacon until crisp. Remove bacon to drain on paper towels; reserve 2 teaspoons drippings in skillet. Add onion, celery, red pepper and garlic to drippings in skillet and sauté 3 minutes, or until softened. Stir in remaining ingredients; bring to a boil over high heat. Cover pan; remove from heat and let stand 5 minutes, or until rice is tender. Garnish with crumbled bacon. Serves 4.

Dawn Henning
Gooseberry Patch

A quick & easy take on the traditional Hoppin' John.

Speedy & Satisfying

Reuben Soup

2 T. butter
1 onion, chopped
4 c. chicken broth
1 c. sauerkraut, drained and chopped
1 bay leaf
2 T. cornstarch
1/4 c. cold water
1 c. whipping cream
1 c. half-and-half
1 lb. deli corned beef, cubed
1 c. shredded Swiss cheese
salt and white pepper to taste
Garnish: rye croutons

Melt butter in a medium saucepan. Add onion and cook until soft. Add broth, sauerkraut and bay leaf. Cover; reduce heat and simmer for 15 minutes. In a small bowl, mix cornstarch and water. Add to saucepan; stir in cream, half-and-half, corned beef and cheese. Simmer over very low heat for 10 to 15 minutes, stirring often; do not boil. Remove bay leaf and add salt and pepper. Ladle into bowls and sprinkle with croutons. Serves 6.

Au Gratin Sausage Skillet

- 16-oz. pkg. Kielbasa sausage, halved lengthwise and cut into 1/2-inch slices
- 2 T. oil
- 5-1/4 oz. pkg. au gratin potato mix
- 2-1/2 c. water
- 2 c. frozen mixed vegetables
- 2 c. shredded Cheddar cheese

In a skillet over medium heat, cook sausage in oil until lightly golden; drain. Add potatoes with contents of sauce mix. Stir in water. Cover and cook for 18 minutes, stirring often. Add vegetables; cover and cook for 5 minutes, or until vegetables are tender. Sprinkle with cheese. Remove from heat; cover and let stand until cheese is melted. Serves 4.

Schinken Nudeln

Christine Middleton
Nicholson, PA

German ham and noodles...mmm, mmm! Delicious with or without catsup.

16-oz. pkg. spaghetti, uncooked
2 T. olive oil
2 T. butter
1 onion, finely chopped
1/2 lb. cooked ham, cut into bite-size cubes
Optional: 1/4 lb. bacon, chopped
salt and pepper to taste
1/4 t. dried oregano
1/4 t. dried basil
1/2 t. dried parsley
2 eggs, beaten
Optional: catsup

Cook spaghetti according to package directions; drain. Meanwhile, heat oil and butter in a large skillet. Sauté onion until translucent; add ham and bacon, if using. Cook until meat is done; quickly stir in seasonings. Remove ham mixture from skillet and keep warm. Add spaghetti to skillet; top with ham mixture. Let fry without stirring until spaghetti turns golden on bottom. Stir from bottom, mixing everything together; fry until heated through. Just before serving, reduce heat to low and pour in eggs. Stir and cook 3 to 5 minutes, until eggs are cooked. Serve with catsup, if desired. Makes 6 servings.

Hot Chinese Chicken Salad

Mary Kay Hahn
Willoughby, OH

This salad comes from my godmother. The grease- and water-stained copy I use is over forty years old!

- 4 to 6 boneless, skinless chicken breasts, cut into 1-inch cubes
- 1/4 c. cornstarch
- 1/2 c. oil
- 1/8 t. garlic powder
- 1 tomato, cubed
- 4-oz. can sliced water chestnuts, drained
- 1/2 c. green onions, chopped
- 1 c. celery, sliced diagonally into 1/2-inch pieces
- 1/4 c. soy sauce
- 2 c. lettuce, finely chopped
- Optional: cooked rice
- Garnish: chow mein or rice noodles

In a bowl, toss chicken with cornstarch. Heat oil in a skillet over high heat. Add chicken and stir-fry until lightly golden. Sprinkle with garlic powder. Stir in tomato, water chestnuts, onions and celery. Stir in soy sauce. Cover; reduce heat and simmer 5 minutes. In a serving bowl, lightly toss chicken and vegetables with lettuce. Serve over rice, if desired; top with garnish. Serves 4 to 6.

Speedy & Satisfying

Stuffed Corn Bake

Laurel Perry
Loganville, GA

Great as a side dish with chicken or beef...and just right for Sunday dinner.

14-3/4 oz. can creamed corn
15-1/4 oz. can corn, drained
1/2 c. butter, melted
6-oz. pkg. chicken-flavored stuffing mix
1/2 c. water
1/2 t. garlic powder
1/2 t. pepper

In a bowl, combine all ingredients and stir until mixed well. Spoon into a greased 2-quart casserole dish. Bake, uncovered, at 350 degrees for 30 minutes. Serves 4 to 6.

Scott's Salisbury Steak

Memory Frost
Greencastle, IN

My husband's original recipe...easy, warm and satisfying.

2 lbs. ground beef
1 onion, diced
2 eggs, beaten
1 sleeve saltine crackers, crushed
2 t. Worcestershire sauce
garlic powder to taste
16-oz. pkg. sliced mushrooms
1 T. butter
3 10-3/4 oz. cans cream of mushroom soup
1 c. sour cream with chives
Optional: cooked egg noodles

In a bowl, mix together ground beef, onion, eggs, crackers, Worcestershire sauce and garlic powder. Form into 8 patties; brown in a skillet over medium heat. Drain patties. Meanwhile, in a separate skillet, sauté mushrooms in butter until tender. Spoon mushrooms on top of patties. In a bowl, mix soup and sour cream; pour over patties. Cook over medium-low heat until patties are done. Serve over noodles, if desired. Serves 6 to 8.

Black Bean & Rice Enchiladas

1 green pepper, chopped
1/4 c. onion, chopped
3 cloves garlic, minced
1 T. olive oil
15-oz. can black beans, drained and rinsed
14-1/4 oz. can diced tomatoes with green chiles
1/4 c. taco sauce
1 T. chili powder
1 t. ground cumin
1/4 t. red pepper flakes
2 c. cooked brown rice
8 10-inch flour tortillas
1 c. salsa
1 c. shredded Cheddar cheese
3 T. fresh cilantro, chopped

In a skillet, sauté green pepper, onion and garlic in oil until tender. Add beans, tomatoes, taco sauce and seasonings. Simmer until heated through and mixture thickens. Add rice; cook 5 minutes. Spoon filling down the center of each tortilla. Roll up tortillas; place in a lightly greased 13"x9" baking pan. Spoon salsa over tortillas. Bake, covered, at 350 degrees for 25 minutes. Uncover; sprinkle with cheese and cilantro. Bake an additional 3 minutes, until cheese is melted. Makes 8 servings.

Bouillabaisse Gumbo

Myrna Salmon
Montrose, CO

I've had this delicious recipe for over thirty years. If you like seafood, you'll love this! Serve with French bread or cornbread.

16-oz. can stewed tomatoes with jalapeños
10-3/4 oz. can tomato soup
10-3/4 oz. can chicken gumbo soup
3 c. water
1 c. sweet potato, peeled and chopped
1/4 c. celery, chopped
1/4 c. carrots, peeled and chopped
1/3 c. green onions, chopped
1 T. fresh parsley, chopped
1 T. fresh cilantro, chopped
1 T. Worcestershire sauce
1 clove garlic, minced
1 bay leaf
1/2 lb. uncooked medium shrimp, cleaned
8-oz. can minced clams
1/4 to 1/2 t. dried oregano
salt and pepper to taste

In a large pot, combine all ingredients except shrimp, clams, oregano, salt and pepper. Cover and simmer over medium-low heat for 30 minutes, or until vegetables are tender. Add shrimp and undrained clams; simmer 10 minutes. Stir in remaining ingredients. Remove bay leaf before serving. Serves 6 to 8.

Spanish-Style Round Steak

Gaynor Simmons
Hemet, CA

Thirty-five years ago when my children were little, I put this together with what I had in my pantry. They still request it!

- 1-1/2 lbs. beef round steak or stew beef, cubed
- 2 T. olive oil
- 1/2 c. onion, chopped
- 1 clove garlic, minced
- 12-oz. can cocktail vegetable juice
- 10-1/2 oz. can beef broth
- 1-1/2 c. water
- 1-1/2 t. salt
- 1/4 t. pepper
- 1-1/2 c. long-cooking rice, uncooked
- 10-oz. pkg. frozen peas
- 1/4 c. chopped pimentos

In a skillet, brown beef in oil. Add onion and garlic; cook and stir until onion is tender. Drain; stir in vegetable juice, broth, water, salt and pepper. Bring to a boil. Cover; reduce heat and simmer 30 minutes. Add rice, peas and pimentos. Return to a boil. Cover; reduce heat and simmer an additional 20 minutes, or until rice is tender. Serves 6 to 8.

Meatless Stuffed Peppers

2 c. cooked brown rice
3 tomatoes, chopped
1 c. frozen corn, thawed
1 sweet onion, chopped
1/3 c. canned kidney beans, drained and rinsed
1/3 c. canned black beans, drained and rinsed
3/4 c. Monterey Jack cheese, cubed
4-1/4 oz. can chopped black olives, drained
3 cloves garlic, minced
1 t. salt
1/2 t. pepper
6 green, red or yellow peppers, tops removed
3/4 c. spaghetti sauce
1/2 c. water

In a large bowl, combine rice, tomatoes, corn, onion and beans. Stir in cheese, olives, garlic, salt and pepper. Spoon into peppers. Combine spaghetti sauce and water. Pour half of sauce mixture into an oval 6-quart slow cooker. Place stuffed peppers on top. Pour remaining sauce over peppers. Cover and cook on low setting for 3-1/2 to 4 hours, until peppers are tender. Makes 6 servings.

Rhonda Reeder
Ellicott City, MD

My pals from card club rave about these delicious peppers! They cook best in an oval slow cooker.

Texas Hominy

Darlene McAdams
Nampa, ID

My family is from Texas and I never get to enjoy hominy unless I make it. It's a great potluck dish or as a side to grilled or barbecued meats!

6 slices bacon, diced
1 onion, finely diced
1 jalapeño, minced
2 cloves garlic, minced
4 15-1/2 oz. cans white hominy, drained
salt and pepper to taste
1-1/2 c. shredded Cheddar cheese, divided
1-1/2 c. shredded Monterey Jack cheese, divided
1/2 c. green onion tops, chopped

In a skillet over medium heat, cook bacon until crisp. Remove bacon to drain on paper towels; reserve drippings in skillet. Sauté onion and jalapeño in reserved drippings until tender. Add garlic and cook one to 2 minutes longer. Stir in hominy, salt and pepper. Remove from heat; stir in one cup each of Cheddar and Monterey Jack cheeses. Spoon into a greased 13"x9" baking pan; sprinkle with remaining cheeses, bacon and green onion tops. Bake, uncovered, at 375 degrees for 30 minutes. Makes 10 servings.

Meatloaf Mexicana

1 lb. ground pork
3/4 lb. lean ground beef
1-1/4 c. shredded Monterey Jack cheese, divided
1 c. dry bread crumbs
1/2 c. taco sauce
2 eggs, beaten
1 T. fresh parsley, chopped
2 t. jalapeños, diced
1 t. salt
Garnish: chopped tomatoes and green onions

Combine pork, beef, one cup cheese, and remaining ingredients except garnish in a large bowl. Press into a lightly greased 9"x5" loaf pan. Bake, uncovered, at 350 degrees for 55 to 60 minutes, until no longer pink in center. Top with remaining cheese and garnishes. Serves 6.

Jo Ann

Serve alongside zesty refried beans and a warm slice of cornbread!

Bratwurst & Potato Salad

6 bratwurst
1/4 c. bacon drippings or oil
2 lbs. redskin potatoes, quartered and boiled
1 bunch green onions, thinly sliced
1/2 c. olive oil
3 T. white wine vinegar
2 T. German mustard
salt and pepper to taste
Optional: 1/8 t. sugar

Cook bratwurst according to package instructions; brown in bacon drippings or oil. Cut into one-inch pieces. Combine bratwurst, potatoes and onions in a large bowl; set aside. Mix together remaining ingredients; pour over bratwurst mixture and toss to coat. Refrigerate 7 to 8 hours, or overnight. Serves 6 to 8.

German-Style Short Ribs

3 lbs. beef short ribs
2 T. oil
10-1/2 oz. can French onion soup
1 c. water
1 T. lemon juice
1/4 t. ground cloves
1/4 t. pepper
2 to 3 slices pumpernickel bread, crumbled
cooked rice or egg noodles

In a large soup pot over medium heat, brown ribs in oil for 6 to 8 minutes; drain. Add soup, water, lemon juice and seasonings; bring to a boil. Cover and reduce heat to low. Simmer for 1-1/2 to 2 hours, stirring occasionally. Stir in bread and serve over rice or noodles. Serves 4.

Easy Lemon-Lime Ham

3 to 4-lb. boneless fully-cooked ham
12-oz. can lemon-lime soda
1/4 c. honey
1/2 t. dry mustard
1/2 t. ground cloves
1/4 t. cinnamon

Place ham in a slow cooker and add soda. Cover and cook on low setting for 6 to 8 hours, or on high setting for 3 to 4 hours. About 30 minutes before serving, combine 3 tablespoons drippings from slow cooker with honey and spices. Mix well and spread over ham. Cover and continue cooking on low setting for final 30 minutes. Remove to a platter; let stand for 15 minutes before slicing. Makes 12 to 16 servings.

Peachy-Keen Sweet Potatoes

Tori Willis
Champaign, IL

The addition of peach pie filling makes these potatoes extra delicious.

2 lbs. sweet potatoes, peeled and cubed
1 c. peach pie filling
2 T. butter, melted
1/4 t. salt
1/4 t. pepper

Place sweet potatoes in a slow cooker that has been sprayed with non-stick vegetable spray. Add remaining ingredients; mix well. Cover and cook on low setting for 5 to 7 hours, until potatoes are tender when pierced with a fork. Serves 8 to 10.

Cornbread Chicken Pot Pie

Roberta Valella
Minot, ND

I made this pot pie when I was out of biscuit baking mix. All I had were two boxes of cornbread mix for a topping. It was a smashing success!

- 4 boneless, skinless chicken breasts, cooked and cubed
- 2 10-3/4 oz. cans cream of chicken soup
- 16-oz. container sour cream
- pepper to taste
- 1 t. dried basil
- 16-oz. pkg. frozen mixed vegetables
- 2 8-1/2 oz. pkgs. cornbread mix
- 1 c. shredded Cheddar cheese

Evenly arrange chicken in a greased 13"x9" baking pan. In a bowl, mix together soup, sour cream, pepper and basil. Add frozen vegetables; spread over chicken in pan. Prepare cornbread mixes according to package directions; spread batter evenly to cover vegetable mixture. Sprinkle with cheese. Bake, uncovered, at 425 degrees for 25 minutes, or until golden and bubbly. Let cool for 15 minutes. Serves 4 to 6.

White Lasagna

Molly Ebert
Decatur, IN

This is my go-to vegetarian dish, but you sure don't have to be a vegetarian to enjoy it. The mushrooms give it a satisfying meaty taste.

8-oz. pkg. lasagna noodles, uncooked
3 T. butter
1 t. lemon juice
16-oz. pkg. sliced mushrooms
1/4 c. all-purpose flour
1 t. salt
1/8 t. cayenne pepper
2-1/2 c. milk
2 T. fresh parsley, chopped
16-oz. container ricotta or cottage cheese
1/2 c. grated Parmesan cheese

Cook lasagna according to package directions; drain. Meanwhile, melt butter in a large skillet over medium heat. Stir in lemon juice and sauté mushrooms until tender. Stir in flour, salt and cayenne pepper. Gradually stir in milk. Cook until slightly thickened; stir in parsley. Spread half the mushroom mixture in a lightly greased 13"x9" baking pan. Alternate layers of noodles and ricotta, ending with ricotta. Top with remaining mushroom mixture. Sprinkle with Parmesan cheese. Bake, covered, at 350 degrees for 45 minutes. Let stand 15 minutes before serving. Makes 10 servings.

Chicken Cordon Bleu

Debi Gilpin
Sharpsburg, GA

Prepare the chicken rolls and refrigerate overnight...in the morning, just pop 'em in the slow cooker and go!

4 to 6 boneless, skinless chicken breasts
4 to 6 thin slices deli ham
4 to 6 slices Swiss cheese
10-3/4 oz. can cream of mushroom soup
1/4 c. milk

Place each chicken breast in a large plastic zipping bag; pound to flatten. Top each with a slice of ham and a slice of cheese; roll up and secure with a toothpick. Arrange rolls in a slow cooker in layers. Mix soup and milk; pour over chicken. Cover and cook on low setting for 4 to 6 hours, until chicken is no longer pink inside. To serve, remove toothpicks and arrange chicken rolls on serving plate; spoon sauce from slow cooker over rolls. Makes 4 to 6 servings.

Garlic Parmesan Chicken

1 sleeve round buttery crackers, crushed
1/2 c. grated Parmesan cheese
1 t. salt
1 t. garlic powder
4 boneless, skinless chicken breasts
1/2 c. sour cream
1/3 c. butter, melted

In a bowl, combine cracker crumbs, Parmesan cheese, salt and garlic powder. Pat chicken breasts dry. Using a pastry brush, coat both sides of each chicken breast in sour cream. Dredge chicken in cracker mixture. Place in a lightly greased 9"x9" baking pan. Drizzle melted butter over chicken. Bake, uncovered, at 350 degrees for 45 minutes, or until juices run clear and chicken is golden. Makes 4 servings.

Crisp Celery-Pear Salad

Stephanie Mayer
Portsmouth, VA

A wonderful cool-weather salad...makes a delicious lunch too.

4 stalks celery, halved lengthwise
2 T. cider vinegar
2 T. honey
1/4 t. salt
2 red pears, cored and diced
8-oz. pkg. white Cheddar cheese, diced
pepper to taste
1/2 c. chopped pecans, toasted

Place celery in a bowl of ice water for 15 minutes. Drain celery and pat dry; slice 1/2-inch thick. Whisk together vinegar, honey and salt in a serving bowl. Add pears; gently stir to coat. Add celery and remaining ingredients; stir to combine. Serve at room temperature. If desired, make up to 2 hours ahead, reserving pecans. Chill; stir in pecans at serving time. Makes 6 servings.

Slow-Cooker Turkey Breast

1/4 c. butter, softened
3 T. fresh sage, chopped
3 T. fresh rosemary, chopped
3 T. fresh thyme, chopped
salt and pepper to taste
6-lb. turkey breast
1 to 2 onions, chopped
3 cloves garlic, pressed
1/2 c. red or white wine or chicken broth
1/2 c. chicken broth

In a bowl, combine butter, herbs, salt and pepper. Rub mixture over turkey breast. Place onion and garlic in a large oval slow cooker. Arrange turkey breast on top. Add wine, if using, and broth. Cover and cook on low setting for 8 to 10 hours, or on high setting for 4 to 5 hours. Serves 8 to 10.

Chicken Comfort Casserole

- 1 c. quick-cooking rice, uncooked
- 10-3/4 oz. can Cheddar cheese soup
- 10-3/4 oz. can cream of chicken soup
- 1/2 c. chicken broth
- 4 c. cooked chicken, chopped
- 16-oz. pkg. frozen chopped broccoli, thawed
- 1/2 c. milk
- 1/4 c. butter, sliced
- 1/2 c. onion, chopped
- salt and pepper to taste
- 1 c. shredded Cheddar cheese

In a bowl, combine rice, soups, broth, chicken and broccoli. Stir in milk, butter and onion. Season with salt and pepper. Mixture will be thick. Spread into an ungreased 11"x7" baking dish; sprinkle with cheese. Bake, covered, at 350 degrees for 30 minutes. Uncover and bake an additional 10 minutes. Let stand 10 minutes before serving. Serves 6 to 8.

Erin Brock
Charleston, WV

Don't like broccoli? Try a bag of your favorite frozen veggies.

Golden Parmesan Roasted Potatoes

1/4 c. all-purpose flour
1/4 c. grated Parmesan cheese
3/4 t. salt
1/8 t. pepper
6 potatoes, peeled and cut into wedges
1/3 c. butter, melted
Garnish: fresh parsley, chopped

Place flour, cheese, salt and pepper in a large plastic zipping bag; mix well. Add potato wedges; shake to coat. Pour butter into a 13"x9" baking pan, tilting to coat; arrange potatoes in pan. Bake, uncovered, at 375 degrees for one hour. Sprinkle with parsley. Serves 4 to 6.

Bread Bowl Beef Stew

1 t. oil
1 lb. boneless top sirloin steak, cubed
3/4 t. garlic salt
1/4 t. pepper
.87-oz. pkg. brown gravy mix
1-1/3 c. water
2 to 3 potatoes, peeled, cooked and quartered
9-oz. pkg. frozen baby carrots, thawed and drained
1-1/2 c. frozen sweet peas, thawed and drained
1 c. canned whole pearl onions, drained
8-oz. tube refrigerated large buttermilk biscuits, at room temperature

Heat oil in a skillet over medium-high heat. Add beef and cook until browned. Add garlic salt, pepper, dry gravy mix and water. Bring to a boil, stirring constantly. Add vegetables. Simmer 5 minutes; set aside. Separate biscuits and flatten to 5-1/2 inch rounds. Press firmly into 8 greased jumbo muffin cups, forming a 1/4-inch rim. Spoon 3/4 cup beef mixture into each cup. Bake, uncovered, at 350 degrees for 14 minutes. Cover with aluminum foil and bake an additional 8 minutes. Makes 8 servings.

Garlicky Green Chili

3 lbs. boneless pork chops, cubed
2 T. oil
1/4 c. all-purpose flour
2 T. garlic, minced
salt and pepper to taste
2 4-oz. cans diced green chiles
14-1/2 oz. can chicken broth
16-oz. jar chunky salsa
1 bunch fresh cilantro, chopped
1 t. ground cumin

In a Dutch oven over medium heat, brown pork in oil. Mix in flour; stir for one minute. Add garlic, salt and pepper; cook for 2 minutes. Stir in remaining ingredients; cover and simmer for 45 minutes. Serves 8.

Autumn Apple-Pecan Dressing

4 c. soft bread cubes
1 c. saltine crackers, crushed
1-1/2 c. apples, peeled, cored, and chopped
1 c. chopped pecans
1 c. onion, chopped
1 c. celery, chopped
2/3 c. chicken broth
1/4 c. butter, melted
2 eggs, beaten
1/2 t. pepper
1/2 t. dried sage

Combine bread cubes, cracker crumbs, apples, pecans, onion and celery in a slow cooker; set aside. In a small bowl, mix remaining ingredients until well blended. Pour into slow cooker and toss to coat. Cover and cook on low setting for 4 to 5 hours, until dressing is puffed and golden around the edges. Serves 8.

Deep-Dish Sausage Pizza

Kathleen Sturm
Corona, CA

Why go out to a pizza parlor, when you can feast on a hot, hearty pizza right from your own kitchen? It's chock-full of the great Italian flavors we love.

- 16-oz. pkg. frozen bread dough, thawed
- 1 lb. sweet Italian pork sausage, casings removed
- 2 c. shredded mozzarella cheese
- 1 green pepper, diced
- 1 red pepper, diced
- 28-oz. can diced tomatoes, drained
- 3/4 t. dried oregano
- 1/2 t. salt
- 1/4 t. garlic powder
- 1/2 c. grated Parmesan cheese

Press dough into the bottom and up the sides of a greased 13"x9" baking pan; set aside. In a large skillet, crumble sausage and cook until no longer pink; drain. Sprinkle sausage over dough; top with mozzarella cheese. In the same skillet, sauté peppers until slightly tender. Stir in tomatoes and seasonings; spoon over pizza. Sprinkle with Parmesan cheese. Bake, uncovered, at 350 degrees for 25 to 35 minutes, until crust is golden. Makes 8 servings.

Cranberry Chicken

Lisa Robason
Corpus Christi, TX

This is a family-favorite, quick-fix recipe for busy holiday evenings.

8-oz. can whole-berry cranberry sauce
1 c. French salad dressing
1.35-oz. pkg. onion soup mix
8 boneless, skinless chicken breasts
1/4 t. pepper
4 c. cooked rice
Optional: fresh parsley

In a bowl, combine cranberry sauce, salad dressing and soup mix. Spread half of the cranberry mixture into a greased 13"x9" baking pan. Arrange chicken in a single layer over sauce mixture; season with pepper, then top with remaining cranberry mixture. Bake, covered, at 325 degrees for 35 to 45 minutes, until juices run clear when chicken is pierced. Serve over cooked rice and garnish with parsley, if desired. Serves 8.

Divine Casserole

Tiffany Brinkley
Broomfield, CO

I like this satisfying casserole with buttery, whipped potatoes...comfort food!

8-oz. pkg. egg noodles, uncooked and divided
1 lb. ground beef
6-oz. can tomato paste
1 t. Worcestershire sauce
1/4 t. hot pepper sauce
1/8 t. dried oregano
1 onion, chopped
1/2 c. plus 2 T. butter, melted and divided
8-oz. container small-curd cottage cheese
1/2 c. sour cream
1/2 c. cream cheese, softened

Cook noodles according to package directions; drain. Meanwhile, brown beef in a skillet over medium heat; drain. Stir in tomato paste, sauces and oregano; set aside. In a separate skillet, sauté onion in 2 tablespoons butter until tender; place in a bowl. Blend in cottage cheese, sour cream and cream cheese. Place half the noodles in an ungreased 2-quart casserole dish. Drizzle with 1/4 cup melted butter; spread with cheese mixture. Toss remaining noodles with remaining butter; spread over cheese mixture. Top with beef mixture. Bake, uncovered, at 350 degrees for 40 minutes. Serves 4 to 6.

Bacon Cheeseburger Casserole

Sandy Schnepf
Le Mars, IA

Topped with French fries, this easy-to-assemble meal will make the whole family happy.

2 lbs. ground beef
1/2 t. salt
1/2 t. pepper
1/2 t. garlic salt
10-3/4 oz. can cream of mushroom soup
10-3/4 can Cheddar cheese soup
1/2 lb. bacon, crisply cooked and crumbled
1/2 onion, thinly sliced
28-oz. pkg. frozen zesty French fries

In a skillet, brown ground beef with seasonings; drain. Stir in soups and bacon. Spread mixture into a 13"x9" baking pan sprayed with non-stick vegetable spray. Layer onion and frozen fries over top. Bake, uncovered, at 350 degrees for 45 to 60 minutes. Makes 10 servings.

The Best Pot Roast Ever

2 c. water
5 to 6-lb. beef pot roast
1-oz. pkg. ranch salad dressing mix
.7-oz. pkg. Italian salad dressing mix
.87-oz. pkg. brown gravy mix
6 to 8 potatoes, peeled and cubed
8 to 10 carrots, peeled and thickly sliced

Pour water into a large oval slow cooker; add roast. Combine mixes and sprinkle over roast. Cover and cook on low setting for 6 to 7 hours; add potatoes and carrots during the last 2 hours of cooking. Serves 6 to 8.

Zucchini Brownies

Vicki Nelson
Puyallup, WA

My mother gave me this recipe years ago after I married and started growing a garden. Like everyone else, I was always looking for ways to use up zucchini.

2 c. all-purpose flour
1 t. salt
1/3 c. baking cocoa
1-1/2 t. baking soda
1-1/4 c. sugar
1/2 c. oil
1 egg, beaten
2 c. zucchini, grated
Garnish: chocolate frosting or powdered sugar

In a bowl, stir together flour, salt, cocoa and baking soda. Mix in sugar, oil, egg and zucchini. Spread into a lightly greased 15"x10" jelly-roll pan. Bake at 350 degrees for 20 minutes. Let cool; garnish as desired. Cut into squares. Makes about 1-1/2 dozen.

Sweet Strawberry Bread

3 c. all-purpose flour
1 t. baking soda
1 t. salt
1-1/2 t. cinnamon
2 c. sugar
4 eggs
1-1/2 c. oil
2 c. strawberries, hulled and sliced
1-1/4 c. chopped walnuts

In a large bowl, combine flour, baking soda, salt, cinnamon and sugar. Add eggs, one at a time, beating well after each addition. Stir in oil; mix in remaining ingredients. Divide batter between 2 greased and floured 9"x5" loaf pans. Bake at 350 degrees for one hour. Makes 2 loaves.

Chocolate Rolls

3/4 c. plus 2 T. all-purpose flour
1/4 c. sugar
2 T. baking cocoa
1/4 t. salt
4 eggs
1 c. milk
2 T. butter, melted and slightly cooled
1/2 t. vanilla extract
Garnish: powdered sugar

In a bowl, sift together flour, sugar, cocoa and salt. Set aside. In a separate bowl, beat eggs for one minute. Beat in milk, butter and vanilla. Beat in flour mixture until smooth. Divide batter among 6 greased popover cups or 12 greased muffin cups; set on a 15"x10" jelly-roll pan. Bake at 375 degrees for 50 minutes. Immediately remove to a wire rack. Sprinkle with powdered sugar. Serve immediately. Makes 1-1/2 to 2 dozen.

Apple Blush Pie

5 apples, peeled, cored and sliced
3/4 c. sugar
15-1/4 oz. can crushed pineapple
1/3 c. red cinnamon candies
2 T. instant tapioca, uncooked
3 T. butter, softened
2 9-inch pie crusts

In a bowl, combine all ingredients except crusts. Place one crust in a 9" pie plate; top with apple mixture. Cut remaining crust into 1/2-inch strips; form a lattice pattern over filling. Bake at 425 degrees for 10 minutes. Reduce temperature to 350 degrees and bake an additional 30 minutes. Let cool. Serves 8.

Katherine Barrett
Bellevue, WA

This recipe goes back about eighty years in my family. It was always made with apples from the trees in our yard.

Almond Amaretto Bread Pudding

Judy Lange
Imperial, PA

My daughter-in-law's mother shared this recipe with me and it is by far my favorite bread pudding ever!

1 qt. half-and-half
1 loaf Italian bread, cubed
3 eggs
1-1/2 c. sugar
2 T. almond extract
1 c. golden raisins
3/4 c. sliced almonds

In a large bowl, pour half-and-half over bread and stir gently. Cover and refrigerate 30 minutes to one hour. In a separate bowl, beat eggs until they begin to foam. Add sugar, mixing well. Stir in almond extract, raisins and almonds. Add to bread mixture and mix well. Pour into a lightly greased 13"x9" baking pan. Bake, uncovered, at 325 degrees for 50 minutes. Serve warm with Amaretto Sauce. Serves 12.

Amaretto Sauce:

1/2 c. butter
1 c. powdered sugar
1/4 c. amaretto liqueur, or
  1 T. almond extract plus
  3 T. water
1 egg, beaten

Melt butter in a double boiler. Beat in remaining ingredients. Cook, stirring constantly, until mixture begins to thicken.

Tropical Carrot Cake

18-oz. pkg. carrot cake mix
1/2 c. water
1/2 c. oil
4 eggs, beaten
8-oz. can crushed pineapple
1/2 c. chopped nuts
1/2 c. sweetened flaked coconut
1/2 c. raisins
16-oz. container cream cheese frosting

In a bowl, beat together dry cake mix, water, oil, eggs and pineapple with juice. Beat with an electric mixer on medium speed for 2 minutes. Stir in nuts, coconut and raisins. Grease and flour the bottoms only of two, 8" round cake pans. Pour batter into pans. Bake at 350 degrees 30 to 35 minutes, until a toothpick inserted in center comes out clean. Cool in pans 10 minutes. Remove to a wire rack to cool completely. Fill layers and frost with frosting. Makes 12 servings.

Baked & Buttery

Pretzel Twists

2 16-oz. loaves frozen bread dough, thawed
1 egg white, beaten
1 t. water
coarse salt to taste

Divide dough into twenty-four, 1-1/2 inch balls. Roll each ball into a rope 14 inches long. Shape as desired; arrange one inch apart on lightly greased baking sheets. Let rise in a warm place for 20 minutes. Whisk together egg white and water; brush over pretzels. Sprinkle with salt. Place a shallow pan with one inch of boiling water on bottom rack of oven. Bake pretzels on rack above water at 350 degrees for 20 minutes, or until golden. Makes 2 dozen.

Raspberry Upside-Down Cake

Marian Buckley
Fontana, CA

Never a fan of pineapple, I did a little dance of joy when a friend made this variation for me!

1/4 c. butter, melted
1/4 c. sugar
1-1/2 c. raspberries
2 T. sliced almonds
1-1/2 c. biscuit baking mix
1/2 c. sugar
1/2 c. milk
2 T. oil
1/2 t. vanilla extract
1/2 t. almond extract
1 egg, beaten
Garnish: additional raspberries and sliced almonds

Drizzle butter in a 9" round cake pan; sprinkle sugar over top. Arrange raspberries, open ends up, over sugar mixture; sprinkle with almonds. In a bowl, combine remaining ingredients except garnish. Beat with an electric mixer on medium speed for 4 minutes. Pour into pan. Bake at 350 degrees for 35 to 40 minutes, until a toothpick tests clean. Immediately place a heatproof serving plate upside-down over pan; turn plate and pan over. Leave pan over cake for one minute to allow sugar mixture to drizzle over cake; remove pan. Cool 10 minutes before serving. Garnish as desired and serve warm. Makes 9 servings.

Brown Sugar Puddin' Pies

15-ct. pkg. frozen mini phyllo cups, unbaked
1/2 c. butter, softened
3/4 c. sugar
3/4 c. brown sugar, packed
2 eggs, beaten
1/2 c. half-and-half
1/2 t. vanilla extract
Garnish: nutmeg and whipped topping

Bake mini cups on an ungreased baking sheet at 350 degrees for 4 to 5 minutes; set aside. Beat butter and sugars together until light and fluffy; blend in eggs, half-and-half and vanilla. Spoon into cups; sprinkle tops with nutmeg. Bake at 350 degrees for 15 to 20 minutes, until set. Top with a dollop of whipped topping and a dusting of nutmeg before serving. Makes 15 servings.

Caramel-Filled Chocolate Cookies

1 c. brown sugar, packed
1 c. plus 1 T. sugar, divided
1 c. margarine, softened
2 eggs, beaten
2 t. vanilla extract
2-1/4 c. all-purpose flour
1 t. baking soda
3/4 c. baking cocoa
1 c. chopped pecans, divided
48 chocolate-covered caramels, unwrapped

In a medium bowl, beat brown sugar, one cup sugar and margarine until fluffy. Mix in eggs and vanilla. In another bowl, combine flour, baking soda, cocoa and 1/2 cup pecans; stir into sugar mixture until combined. In a cup, mix remaining pecans and sugar; set aside. For each cookie, shape one tablespoon dough around one caramel. Dip the dough ball, one side only, into the pecan mixture. Place cookies, pecan mixture-side up, on ungreased baking sheets. Bake at 375 degrees for 7 to 10 minutes. Cool on baking sheets 2 minutes; remove to a wire rack to cool completely. Makes 4 dozen.

Pecan Pie Muffins

1 c. light brown sugar, packed
1/2 c. all-purpose flour
2 eggs, beaten
2/3 c. butter, melted
1 c. chopped pecans
Optional: pecan halves

In a bowl, stir together all ingredients except pecan halves. Fill greased mini muffin cups 2/3 full. Top each with a pecan half, if using. Bake at 350 degrees for 12 to 15 minutes, until golden. Makes 2-1/2 to 3 dozen.

Sandy Glennen
Dandridge, TN

Perfectly nutty and sweet! Oh-so-good with a cup of tea.

Crunchy Oat & Fruit Crisp

1 c. quick-cooking oats, uncooked
3/4 c. brown sugar, packed and divided
5 T. all-purpose flour, divided
1/3 c. margarine, melted
1 c. blueberries
1 c. cherries, pitted
4 apples, peeled, cored and thickly sliced
1/4 c. frozen orange juice concentrate, thawed
1 T. cinnamon

In a bowl, combine oats, 1/2 cup brown sugar, 2 tablespoons flour and margarine; set aside. In a separate bowl, combine fruit, 1/4 cup brown sugar and remaining ingredients. Stir until fruit is evenly coated. Spoon fruit mixture into an ungreased 8"x8" baking pan. Sprinkle oat mixture over top. Bake at 350 degrees for 30 to 35 minutes, until apples are tender and topping is golden. Serves 4 to 6.

Mocha-Oatmeal Cake

A'Lisa Johnson
Abilene, KS

My mom always made this cake for special occasions. After she passed away, I found the recipe in her file and have cherished it ever since!

2 T. instant coffee granules
1-1/3 c. boiling water
1 c. quick-cooking oats, uncooked
3/4 c. plus 1-1/2 T. butter, divided
1 c. sugar
1 c. brown sugar, packed
2 eggs
2 t. vanilla extract, divided
2 c. all-purpose flour
1-1/4 t. baking soda
3/4 t. plus 1/8 t. salt, divided
3 T. baking cocoa
1 c. powdered sugar
1-1/2 T. brewed coffee

Mix coffee granules and water. Stir in oats; let stand 20 minutes. Beat 3/4 cup butter until creamy. Beat in sugars until fluffy. Beat in eggs, one at a time, and 1-1/2 teaspoons vanilla. Blend in oat mixture; set aside. In a separate bowl, combine flour, baking soda, 3/4 teaspoon salt and cocoa. Add flour mixture to butter mixture. Pour into a greased and floured Bundt® pan. Bake at 350 degrees for 50 minutes. Cool in pan 10 minutes; remove from pan to cool on a wire rack. Combine 1-1/2 tablespoons butter, 1/8 teaspoon salt, 1/3 teaspoon vanilla, powdered sugar and brewed coffee; drizzle over cake. Makes 12 servings.

Frosted Cherry Drops

Charlene Sidwell
Altamont, IL

These have always been a favorite of our family. They're perfect for a colorful plate of Christmas cookies, either for home or as a gift.

18-1/2 oz. pkg. white cake mix
1/2 c. sour cream
3 T. maraschino cherry juice
1/4 t. almond extract
1 egg, beaten
1/2 c. maraschino cherries, finely chopped
Garnish: maraschino cherries, quartered

In a bowl, combine dry cake mix, sour cream, cherry juice, almond extract and egg. Fold in chopped cherries. Drop by teaspoonfuls, 2 inches apart, onto ungreased baking sheets. Bake at 350 degrees for 8 to 12 minutes, until edges are lightly golden. Cool one minute on baking sheets; remove to a wire rack to cool completely. Frost with Cherry Frosting; top with cherry quarters. Makes 2-1/2 to 3 dozen.

Cherry Frosting:

2-1/2 c. powdered sugar
1/4 c. margarine, softened
1 T. maraschino cherry juice
2 to 3 T. milk

In a small bowl, combine all ingredients, adding enough milk for desired spreading consistency.

Orange-Peach Dump Cake

14-1/2 oz. can peach pie filling, chopped
18-oz. pkg. orange cake mix
2 eggs, beaten
1/2 c. sour cream
Optional: vanilla ice cream

Combine all ingredients except ice cream in an ungreased 13"x9" baking pan. Mix with a fork until well blended; smooth top with a spatula. Bake at 350 degrees for 40 to 45 minutes. Serve with ice cream, if desired. Serves 8 to 10.

Elizabeth Wenk
Cuyahoga Falls, OH

A different flavor combination of this trusty dessert. Try it with a dollop of whipped topping and a sprinkle of orange zest.

Marshmallow Graham Custard

1-1/2 c. milk
1/3 c. graham cracker crumbs, finely ground
2 eggs, beaten
2 T. sugar
1/8 t. salt
1/2 t. vanilla extract
8 marshmallows, quartered

In a large bowl, pour milk over cracker crumbs; set aside. In a separate bowl, combine eggs, sugar, salt and vanilla; stir into milk mixture. Stir in marshmallows and pour into 4 ungreased custard cups. Set cups in a shallow pan of hot water. Bake at 325 degrees for 40 minutes, or until a knife inserted in the center comes out clean. Makes 4 servings.

Lemon Snowdrops

Brenda Huey
Geneva, IN

These pretty cookies are so good...they melt in your mouth!

2 c. plus 3 T. shortening, divided
1 c. powdered sugar
2 t. lemon extract
1/2 t. salt
4 c. all-purpose flour
2 eggs, beaten
juice and zest of 1 lemon
1-1/3 c. sugar
Garnish: powdered sugar

Mix together 2 cups shortening, powdered sugar, lemon extract and salt; slowly stir in flour until blended. Roll dough into one-inch balls and arrange on ungreased baking sheets. Press a thumbprint into the center of each ball. In a saucepan, combine 3 tablespoons shortening and remaining ingredients except garnish. Cook and stir over low heat until slightly thickened. Spoon one teaspoon filling into each thumbprint. Bake at 325 degrees for 8 to 10 minutes, until lightly golden. Let cool; dust with powdered sugar. Makes 4 to 6 dozen.

Shoo Fly Pie

1 t. baking soda
1 c. hot water
1/2 c. brown sugar, packed
3 eggs, beaten
1 c. molasses
9-inch pie crust

Dissolve baking soda in hot water in a medium bowl. Stir in remaining ingredients except pie crust. Pour half the mixture into pie crust; sprinkle with 3/4 cup Crumb Topping. Repeat layers ending with Crumb Topping. Bake at 400 degrees for 10 minutes. Reduce heat to 375 degrees and bake for an additional 50 minutes. Serves 8.

Crumb Topping:

2-1/2 c. all-purpose flour
1 c. brown sugar, packed
1/2 c. shortening

Combine flour and brown sugar; mix well. Cut in shortening until crumbly.

Peaches & Cream Dessert

3/4 c. all-purpose flour
3-1/2 oz. pkg. instant vanilla pudding mix
1 t. baking powder
1 egg, beaten
1/2 c. milk
3 T. butter, melted and slightly cooled
16-oz. can sliced peaches, drained and 1/3 c. juice reserved
8-oz. pkg. cream cheese, softened
1/2 c. plus 1 T. sugar, divided
1/2 t. cinnamon

In a bowl, combine flour, dry pudding mix and baking powder; set aside. In a separate bowl, blend egg, milk and butter together; add to flour mixture. Mix well; spread in a greased 8"x8" baking pan. Chop peaches and sprinkle over batter; set aside. Blend cream cheese, 1/2 cup sugar and reserved peach juice together until smooth; pour over peaches. Mix remaining sugar and cinnamon together; sprinkle on top. Bake at 350 degrees for 45 minutes. Makes 9 servings.

Beth Ratcliff
West Des Moines, IA

Peaches never tasted so good!

Dark Chocolate Pecan Pie

Rita Morgan
Pueblo, CO

Decadent, rich and fantastic! My husband always saves room for dessert when this is on the menu.

1-1/2 c. pecan halves
1-1/2 c. dark chocolate chips
1 T. all-purpose flour
1/2 c. butter, softened
1/2 c. light brown sugar, packed
3 eggs
1/2 c. dark corn syrup
2 t. vanilla extract
1/4 t. salt
9-inch pie crust, baked
Garnish: whipped topping

In a bowl, stir together pecans, chocolate chips and flour; set aside. In another bowl, beat butter and brown sugar until well blended. Beat in eggs, one at a time. Mix in corn syrup, vanilla and salt, just until blended. Stir in pecan mixture. Pour into baked pie crust. Bake at 325 degrees for 55 to 60 minutes, until a toothpick inserted in center comes out with just melted chocolate. Center will set as it cools. Cool on a wire rack. Chill until serving time. Garnish with whipped topping. Makes 8 servings.

Cornmeal-Cheddar Biscuits

1-1/2 c. all-purpose flour
1/2 c. yellow cornmeal
2 t. sugar
1 T. baking powder
1/4 to 1/2 t. salt
1/2 c. butter, softened
1/2 c. shredded Cheddar cheese
1 c. milk

In a bowl, combine flour, cornmeal, sugar, baking powder and salt; cut in butter until mixture resembles coarse crumbs. Stir in cheese and milk just until moistened. Drop dough by 1/4 cupfuls onto an ungreased baking sheet. Bake at 450 degrees for 12 to 15 minutes, until lightly golden. Makes one dozen.

Pull-Apart Bacon Bread

- 1 t. oil
- 3/4 c. green pepper, chopped
- 3/4 c. onion, chopped
- 3 7-1/2 oz. tubes refrigerated buttermilk biscuits
- 1 lb. bacon, crisply cooked and crumbled
- 1/4 c. margarine, melted
- 1 c. shredded Cheddar cheese

Heat oil in a large skillet; sauté green pepper and onion until tender. Remove from heat; set aside. Slice biscuits into quarters; place in a bowl. Add pepper mixture, bacon, margarine and cheese; toss until mixed. Transfer mixture to a greased 10" tube pan; bake at 350 degrees for 30 minutes. Invert onto a serving platter to serve. Serves 8.

Chocolate Chip Macaroon Bars

1/2 c. butter, softened
1 c. plus 2 T. all-purpose flour, divided
1-1/2 c. brown sugar, packed and divided
2 eggs, beaten
1/4 t. salt
1 c. chopped pecans
1-1/2 c. sweetened flaked coconut
1 t. vanilla extract
1 c. semi-sweet chocolate chips

Mix together butter, one cup flour and 1/2 cup brown sugar. Pat into the bottom of a greased 13"x9" baking pan. Bake at 325 degrees for 15 minutes. In a medium bowl, blend together remaining flour, remaining brown sugar and other ingredients. Spread mixture onto baked crust. Bake for an additional 25 minutes. Let cool and cut into bars. Makes 1-1/2 dozen.

Sheryl Thomas
Potterville, MI

Tuck these in an old-fashioned cookie jar for gift-giving.

Marble Cheesecake

Sharon Dennison
Floyds Knobs, IN

I've been making this cheesecake for years. My family really loves when I bring it to gatherings.

- 1 c. graham cracker crumbs
- 3 T. sugar
- 3 T. margarine, melted
- 3 8-oz. pkgs. cream cheese, softened
- 3/4 c. sugar
- 3 T. all-purpose flour
- 1 t. vanilla extract
- 3 eggs, beaten
- 1-oz. sq. unsweetened baking chocolate, melted and cooled slightly

In a bowl, combine cracker crumbs, sugar and margarine; press into the bottom of a 9" springform pan. Bake at 350 degrees for 10 minutes. With an electric mixer on medium speed, beat cream cheese, sugar, flour and vanilla until well blended. Blend in eggs. Remove one cup of batter to a separate bowl and blend in melted chocolate. Spoon plain and chocolate batters alternately over crust. Use a knife to swirl through batter several times for marble effect. Bake at 450 degrees for 10 minutes. Reduce oven to 250 degrees; bake an additional 30 minutes. Loosen pan's rim, but do not remove. Let cool; remove rim. Chill until serving time. Serves 8 to 10.

Sweet Potato Pie

14-1/2 oz. can sweet potatoes, drained and mashed
3/4 c. milk
3/4 c. brown sugar, packed
2 eggs, beaten
1 T. butter, melted
1/2 t. salt
1/2 t. cinnamon
9-inch pie crust

Combine all ingredients except pie crust in a blender; process until smooth. Pour into crust. Bake at 400 degrees for 10 minutes. Cover edges of crust with aluminum foil. Reduce heat to 350 degrees; bake for an additional 35 minutes, or until a knife tip inserted in center comes out clean. Serves 6 to 8.

Monster Bars

Heidi Ladwig
Odebolt, IA

These are so easy and much less time-consuming than the drop cookie version. We top them with ice cream drizzled with chocolate and caramel syrups.

1/2 c. butter, softened
1 c. brown sugar, packed
1 c. sugar
1-1/2 c. creamy peanut butter
3 eggs, beaten
2 t. vanilla extract
2 t. baking soda
4-1/2 c. quick-cooking oats
1 c. semi-sweet chocolate chips
1 c. candy-coated chocolates

In a bowl, mix together all ingredients in order listed. Spread mixture in a greased 15"x10" jelly-roll pan. Bake at 350 degrees for 15 minutes, or until lightly golden. Let cool and cut into bars. Makes about 1-1/2 dozen.

INDEX

Appetizers

Buffalo Wing Dip, 23
Deluxe Cocktail Sausages, 10
Nacho Chicken Dip, 11
Sandwich on a Stick, 15
Spiced Orange Pecans, 28
Sweet Salsa, 20
Weda's Stuffed Tomatoes, 26

Beverages & Snacks

Game-Time Party Mix, 22
Sangria Punch, 17
Spiced Orange Pecans, 18

Breads

Chocolate Rolls, 84
Cornmeal-Cheddar Biscuits, 102
Pecan Pie Muffins, 92
Pretzel Twists, 88
Pull-Apart Bacon Bread, 103
Sweet Strawberry Bread, 83

Cookies

4-Layer Cookie Bars, 14
Caramel-Filled Chocolate Cookies, 91
Chocolate Chip Macaroon Bars, 104
Frosted Cherry Drops, 95
Lemon Snowdrops, 98
Monster Bars, 107

Desserts

Almond Amaretto Bread Pudding, 86
Apple Blush Pie, 85
Berry Patch Fondue, 27
Brown Sugar Puddin' Pies, 90
Crunchy Oat & Fruit Crisp, 93
Dark Chocolate Pecan Pie, 101
Marble Cheesecake, 105
Marshmallow Graham Custard, 97
Mocha-Oatmeal Cake, 94
Orange-Peach Dump Cake, 96
Peaches & Cream Dessert, 100
Peanut Buttery Chocolatey Cups, 28
Raspberry Upside-Down Cake, 89
Red Velvet Cake Balls, 16
Shoo Fly Pie, 99
Sweet Potato Pie, 106
Tropical Carrot Cake, 87
Zucchini Brownies, 82

Mains

Au Gratin Sausage Skillet, 51
Bacon Cheeseburger Casserole, 80
Bavarian Beef & Noodles, 45
Best Pot Roast Ever, The, 81
Black Bean & Rice Enchiladas, 56
Bowties & Blush, 36
Chicken Comfort Casserole, 72
Chicken Cordon Bleu, 68
Cornbread Chicken Pot Pie, 66
Cranberry Chicken, 78

INDEX

Deep-Dish Sausage Pizza, 77
Dijon Chicken & Fresh Herbs, 42
Divine Casserole, 79
Easy Lemon-Lime Ham, 64
Fancy Crescent Chicken, 35
Farmhouse Chicken Bake, 47
Garlic Parmesan Chicken, 69
German-Style Short Ribs, 63
Hot Chinese Chicken Salad, 53
Meatless Stuffed Peppers, 59
Meatloaf Mexicana, 61
Mom's One-Pot Pork Chop Dinner, 48
Peppers & Pierogies, 31
Ranch Chicken Pizza, 19
Roasted Chicken & Apples, 30
Salmon with Balsamic Sauce, 39
Sam's Sweet-and-Sour Pork, 37
Schinken Nudeln, 52
Scott's Salisbury Steak, 55
Slow-Cooker Turkey Breast, 71
Spanish-Style Round Steak, 58
Speedy Goulash, 46
White Lasagna, 67

Salads

7th-Heaven Layered Salad, 33
Aunt Louise's Salad, 25
Bratwurst & Potato Salad, 62
Corn Chip Salad, 8
Cornbread Salad, 29
Crisp Celery-Pear Salad, 70
Marinated Carrot Salad, 12
Tangy Summer Slaw, 43

Sandwiches

Brown Sugar Barbecue Sandwiches, 21
Easy French Dip Sandwiches, 9
Hot Chicken Sandwiches, 24
Open-Faced Lone Star Burgers, 41
Santa Fe Sandwiches, 7
Tailgate Sandwich Ring, 13

Sides

Autumn Apple-Pecan Dressing, 76
Cajun Oven Fries, 40
Golden Parmesan Roasted Potatoes, 73
Hoppin' Jane, 49
Peachy-Keen Sweet Potatoes, 65
Sassy Squash, 34
Stuffed Corn Bake, 54
Texas Hominy, 60

Soups

Bouillabaisse Gumbo, 57
Bread Bowl Beef Stew, 74
Chicken & Barley Chili, 32
Garlicky Green Chili, 75
Quick & Creamy Vegetable Soup, 38
Reuben Soup, 50
Texas Two-Step in a Jar, 44

Easy French Dip Sandwiches, page 9

Zucchini Brownies, page 82

Cajun Oven Fries, page 40

Sweet Salsa, page 20

Back in 1984, we were next-door neighbors raising our families in the little town of Delaware, Ohio. Two moms with small children, we were looking for a way to do what we loved and stay home with the kids too. We had always shared a love of home cooking and making memories with family & friends and so, after many a conversation over the backyard fence, **Gooseberry Patch** was born.

We put together our first catalog at our kitchen tables, enlisting the help of our loved ones wherever we could. From that very first mailing, we found an immediate connection with many of our customers and it wasn't long before we began receiving letters, photos and recipes from these new friends. In 1992, we put together our very first cookbook, compiled from hundreds of these recipes and, the rest, as they say, is history.

Hard to believe it's been over 25 years since those kitchen-table days! From that original little **Gooseberry Patch** family, we've grown to include an amazing group of creative folks who love cooking, decorating and creating as much as we do. Today, we're best known for our homestyle, family-friendly cookbooks, now recognized as national bestsellers.

Jo Ann & Vickie

One thing's for sure, we couldn't have done it without our friends all across the country. Each year, we're honored to turn thousands of your recipes into our collectible cookbooks. Our hope is that each book captures the stories and heart of all of you who have shared with us. Whether you've been with us since the beginning or are just discovering us, welcome to the **Gooseberry Patch** family!

Visit us online:

www.gooseberrypatch.com

1•800•854•6673

U.S. to Canadian Recipe Equivalents

Volume Measurements

1/4 teaspoon	1 mL
1/2 teaspoon	2 mL
1 teaspoon	5 mL
1 tablespoon = 3 teaspoons	15 mL
2 tablespoons = 1 fluid ounce	30 mL
1/4 cup	60 mL
1/3 cup	75 mL
1/2 cup = 4 fluid ounces	125 mL
1 cup = 8 fluid ounces	250 mL
2 cups = 1 pint =16 fluid ounces	500 mL
4 cups = 1 quart	1 L

Weights

1 ounce	30 g
4 ounces	120 g
8 ounces	225 g
16 ounces = 1 pound	450 g

Oven Temperatures

300° F	150° C
325° F	160° C
350° F	180° C
375° F	190° C
400° F	200° C
450° F	230° C

Baking Pan Sizes

Square

8x8x2 inches	2 L = 20x20x5 cm
9x9x2 inches	2.5 L = 23x23x5 cm

Rectangular

13x9x2 inches	3.5 L = 33x23x5 cm

Loaf

9x5x3 inches	2 L = 23x13x7 cm

Round

8x1-1/2 inches	1.2 L = 20x4 cm
9x1-1/2 inches	1.5 L = 23x4 cm

Recipe Abbreviations

t. = teaspoon
T. = tablespoon
c. = cup
pt. = pint
qt. = quart
gal. = gallon
ltr. = liter
oz. = ounce
lb. = pound
doz. = dozen
pkg. = package
env. = envelope

Kitchen Measurements

A pinch = 1/8 tablespoon
3 teaspoons = 1 tablespoon
2 tablespoons = 1/8 cup
4 tablespoons = 1/4 cup
8 tablespoons = 1/2 cup
16 tablespoons = 1 cup
2 cups = 1 pint
4 cups = 1 quart
4 quarts = 1 gallon

1 fluid ounce = 2 tablespoons
4 fluid ounces = 1/2 cup
8 fluid ounces = 1 cup
16 fluid ounces = 1 pint
32 fluid ounces = 1 quart
16 ounces net weight = 1 pound